THE *SPIRITUAL* JOURNEY

MEMOIRS

of

VIOLA CHANCELLOR

Published and Distributed by
Sharifa Publishing
Henderson, NV 89002
 (310) 435-1080
shazired@yahoo.com

Packaging and Distributed by
Professional Publishing House
1425 W. Manchester Ave., Ste. B
Los Angeles, CA 90047
Email: professionalpublishinghouse@yahoo.com
www.professionalpublishinghouse..com

Cover design: TWA Solutions
First Printing July, 2023
ISBN 979-8-218-24694-5
10987654321

For inquiries contact: shazired@yahoo.com

Dedication

To my mother, the late Lula Bell, for your love of family and for teaching me sustainable values.

To my beautiful daughters, Tammy, Renate, and Heidi Chancellor, and my loving son, Robert Chancellor, for their undying love, help, and patience

To my cousin, the late OC Chatman, for taking me places to see family members that I had not seen.

To my cousin, the late Leonard Jackson. Thanks for taking the time when I came to visit to tell me stories of our family.

Table of Contents

Preface

I believe we are born into time and space for a reason. Keeping all things in perspective, the Universe designated my mother, Lula Bell, and used her as the vehicle which allowed my entrance onto this planet in a little small town called Gadsden in the state of Alabama. From birth to the present time, my ancestors have guided me in my transformation of life's knowledge of self. The marriage union of my parents produced three children. My mother gave birth to four children.

In my spiritual journey I have encountered many obstacles, but God is always there to pick me up when I fall. My journey was laid out for me to be a foot soldier. I feel so blessed. God provided everything I needed to get me where I am now love, kindness, education, shelter, and my ancestors.

It's taken decades to accept that I was different and believe in myself. I'd often ponder the question: who was I?

Chapter 1

MEET MY ANCESTORS

Although I still have some reluctance, there is a greater calling to share my stories in hopes that others who share similar experiences find some guidance or understanding. If this is the reader, you are not alone. From birth to the present time, my ancestors have guided my transformation of life's knowledge of self. They speak to us through the dreams state and there's nothing to fear. Allow this book and experiences encourage an increase in curiosity surrounding what may deem like "haunting" dreams. There is much more at play

It's quite common for my children to alert me of conversations I would have while sleeping. On a few occasions, my daughter video recorded me while sleeping.

As I type this Memoir, the spirits are around me and a rainbow is on the frame of the door.

Since I was a child, my dreams have always been haunting. Deeply coded in my dreams were some relevant truths. At that time, I did not have this awareness. But throughout life, my dreams were found to be premonitions of future events. Most times, these events were unwanted, for decades, I was reluctant to share my experiences, because of not being understood.

On a beautiful fall day, October 30, 2000, I began to document my story including the strange dreams that have accompanied me most of my life. To the best of my ability, I would try to jot down what I could remember in my diary. I would write the dreams on the closest piece of paper that I could find. Unfortunately, I lost many loose papers over the years. However, I continued to maintain the diary, consolidating the trials and tribulations of my hieratic dreams.

One thing for sure is that my spirits have guided and protected me throughout my journey and put me in the place I need to be. As I type this book, I see small rainbows on the frame of the door in my bedroom. This happens sometimes, and I am used to it. It took me to my present time to believe in myself and to understand that I am different. I used to ask myself who I was because I knew I was different, but to what extent?

My dreams that would come true always amazed me, and always had me hollering in my dreams because I was frightened by him hitting me on the top of my head or feet. God has brought me forward, so I am not afraid anymore. My true purpose has not yet been revealed, but I am getting close to that realization. This book was constructed through actual real events of my life experiences. My journey in the great migration from Alabama to the sunshine state of California, landing in the state of Nevada.

The marriage union of my parents produced three children. My mother gave birth to four children. My oldest sister, Katie Mae, took on the Curry surname because my mother was unmarried to her father. The norm during this period was that the father's name did not go on the birth certificate if the parents were not married.

My parents later divorced, and both remarried. From my father's second marriage, he had two daughters. Mary and Belinda, My research was restricted to the family surnames of Wiley, Hall, Lane, McElderry, Curry, Byers, Chancellor, and Gaddis. I spent many hours of research to document this genealogy story properly. However, I will note the inaccuracies.

My research into getting to know my ancestors extended over a period of twenty-five years with many interruptions. The hardest breaking incident occurred when I had not backed up my work and the computer crashed, causing me to lose data. I gathered my sources of information from memory, family members, birth certificates, marriage licenses, social security records, military records, death records, photos, and census reports. Unfortunately, a fire destroyed the 1890 Census Report, thus the loss of data. Through these sources, some of my ancestors have been able to speak to me and tell me something about themselves.

Perhaps my viewing of photos, the census reports and interviews of family members conjured up memories that were buried in my DNA. In my dreams, my ancestors came to me mostly at night when I was sleeping. At first, I was frightened, but the fear subsided to the curiosity of wanting to know who they were.

Because of my passion and due diligence in getting to know my ancestors I was able to gather historical data as to who they were. The Census Report provides information as to their birth, education, where they lived, number of live and deceased children, and when they got married. My research has also led me to be in an Indian Nation

The DNA of my ancestors flows through my blood. They were very strong people who had endured pre and pro slavery (Jim Crow). My grandparents and I spent a lot of time riding up and down on the train from Munford to Gadsden, especially on the weekends.

As a little girl, during the night a lady who had long hair used to stand at the foot of my bed and stare at me. She never said anything, just looked at me and put me in a state of terror. As a result, I would cover my head up. One day many years lady My oldest daughter who had observed me sleeping informed me that the way I slept was considered a peek a boo style of sleeping.

To this day I still cover my head when sleeping. First, I was fearful of the lady, then the man who took over after the lady left and now the groups, more people to frighten me. These ancestors came in hitting me on the head and feet. I always covered my head up only leaving an opening for a breeding space. I would peek to see if the lady was still there. The lady would usually leave before daybreak. I was terrified of this lady who I would wake up to see not talking but standing, looking at me at the foot of my bed. Why I was so afraid since she never touched me, she was there to protect me from the harms of the world and to prepare me for various battles for God. I wasn't intuitively aware of this information. I believe the first two ancestors who came early in life were my grandma and father. Groups came later.

So many things happened to me while becoming the woman I am today. In 1993, I started writing this book. It is now 2023, thirty years later. During this period, so many things have happened that have me questioning who I am.

At this time, most of our older family has transitioned, except for my mother's oldest sister Chanie Jones, who lived to be one hundred two years old. I had to research my ancestry to document this book. To my benefit, I knew most of my family members. We would often visit them in the country. They would also visit us who lived in the city. Having a lady to stand at the foot of my bed and a man chasing me in a dream was one thing, but to have other ancestors appear was entirely another thing. I wanted to know all about them so the things I learned I will share with you

As I began my research, asking questions of the family, young and old, was the beginning of my wonderful experiences with my ancestors. I was doing what I could to know who they were, and they wanted to know who I was. It seemed like my ancestors wanted to come and meet me. Different ones would show up at night. I would get hit; someone would always make noise all around me. It inspired me to maintain a journal to note the unusual dreams and experiences I was encountering on my journey with the spirits of God. I documented my ancestors, from which I came, in this memoir, *The Ancestral Timeline of the Wiley and Curry Family*.

The memories become overwhelming each time I travel to my hometown in the city of Gadsden and the state of Alabama. It is always very emotional for me. Not only do I get to see my friends, but my ancestors would come to visit as well. There would be a certain smell and a wonderful feeling that would come for me. Tears would flow from my eyes as though I were a river. Today I am here for my class reunion and am heading to my hotel room.

It is a blessing to have talked to my parents, grandparents, aunts, uncles, and cousins. I want to introduce them to you. We got our surname, Wiley, from the slave owners. Although the name: Wyley and Wiley are interchangeable, the pronunciation is the same. The males also took on the first name of William, but my father would later change his name from William to Harrison and the spelling of his name from Wiley to Wyley, which is documented in the oldest document that I have: my parents' marriage license, dated December 26, 1926.

My father, Harrison Wiley, was born in Talladega, Alabama, as William Wiley Sr. and the 1920 Census Report listed him as having two sisters: Lillie Mae and Bertha Wiley. My father's parents—my grandparents— were William Wiley and Mary McElderry.

My grandfather was born on November 9, 1887, in Munford, Talladega County, Alabama. The 1910 Census Report listed him as being around seventeen years old and the fifth child of my great-grandparents, William, and Lucinda Wiley. Although the 1910 census listed my grandfather, he does not appear on the 1900 report, as does my grandmother. My grandmother, Mary McElderry, first appeared on the 1900 Census when she was about eight years old.

My grandfather's father, who was also my great-grandfather, was named William M. Wiley and was born about 1858 in the state of Georgia. He lived during the time of slavery, the Civil War, and the death of Abraham Lincoln, the 16th President of the United States of America.

Abraham Lincoln led the Civil War from April 12, 1861, to 1865. My great-grandfather was right in the middle of this very unsettling period. My great-grandmother Lucinda was born about ten years after the war, with 1875 as the estimated year of birth in the state of Georgia.

In 1910, my great-grandfather was documented at fifty-two years old while my grandmother Lucinda was listed at forty years old. William and Lucinda later married. However, there is no data if they individually migrated from Georgia to Alabama or were married before arriving in Alabama.

My great-grandparents, William, and Lucinda, in 1910 had been married for twenty-six years and Lucinda had given birth to eighteen children with only thirteen living. Mary Neil my cousin, identified from the 1910 Census shared with me that my aunt Anna her grandmother had raised her after the death of her mother when she was three years old. Mary Neil also identified my great-aunt Fannie Wiley, who migrated to Chattanooga with her daughter, Barbara Jean. Mary Neil also provided me with an actual physical address. My mother told me that my father had named me after my great-aunt Viola, who lived in Chattanooga.

My cousin Leonard Jackson, whose mother was my father's sister, told me that a lady named Lucinda used to visit the family all the time. He described her as a tall, fair-colored woman that visited them from Chattanooga, Tennessee.

The 1920s brought about changes for my great-grandparents. My great-grandfather William had transitioned to the spirit world, and my great-grandmother Lucinda was now a widow and the head of the household. Whereas some of the children had left the household, four additional children had joined the family. Lucinda gave birth to a total of twenty-two children.

My grandfather William, who was approximately twenty-seven years of age in 1920, had left the household and married my grandmother Mary McElderry who had given birth to three children: Bertha Wiley, Lillie Mae Wiley, and William Wiley, who would become my father. There is no record of my grandfather's parents, my great-grandparents. However, the Census Report reveals that their parents were from Georgia.

My father's mother, Mary McElderry, was born to my great-grandparents Henry McElderry and Sally Lane. Henry estimated birth was during the year of 1867 in Talladega, Alabama, to the parents of Howard and Lucinda McElderry, who were both born into slavery. Henry's father, Howard McElderry, estimated birth was 1921 and his birthplace was listed as North Carolina, but his mother's, Lucinda McElderry, birthplace was listed as Talladega, with an estimated year of birth as 1840.

Because Lucinda's maiden name is unknown, it is difficult to authenticate her before her marriage to Howard McElderry. However, the report indicated that her mother and father's birthplace was in Alabama. Five children had been born to that marriage, as reflected in the 1870 Census Report.

Ten years later, in 1880, one child had left the household and six additional children were born, including a set of twins. My grandfather's parents, Henry, and Lucinda McElderry had a total of ten children.

The 1900 Census Report documented that Henry McElderry had left his parents' household and married Sallie Lane, and to that union, Sally had given birth to four children, which included my grandmother, Mary, who was the second child born to her parents. Documents show they had been married for ten years.

Although Sallie had given birth to six children, only four were living. The 1910 Census Report showed the addition of four children to the household, thereby Sallie gave birth to twelve children and eight were living. The birth of another child was born in the next decade, a girl named Essie Mae, was ten years old on the 1920 Census Report. Before an interview with my cousin, Leonard Jackson, in 2007, Sally Lane was unknown to me. I recall my mother talking about the Lanes as being related to the Wiley family, but she didn't share any names.

Sally Lane was identified by her daughter, Essie Mae, when she acknowledged her mother on her death certificate in 1953.

Per my interview with Arthur McElderry, Essie Mae married Bubba Orr. Therefore, when she signed the death certificate, she signed it as Essie Mae Orr. Upon signing the death certificate, Essie Mae listed Detroit, Michigan, as her place of residence. At that time, Essie Mae was the mother of one child named Roland McElderry.

Sally Lane was the grandmother of my cousin Bernard Gooden.

Arthur McElderry, my cousin, authenticates the Census reports when he identifies that Mary McElderry is his aunt and that her brother, Willie McElderry, was his father. Also, another cousin, Bernard Gooden, identifies my grandmother's sister, Martha, as his mother.

It had been said that there are two sets of Curry's from Talladega and because one set's color tone is lighter than the other that they are not related. Through my interviews we were able to connect and show the family relationship between the Curry's, Goodens, and McElderrys.

My interview with Bernard Gooden reveals that his mother, Martha McElderry, married Gus Gooden. Arthur McElderry, his father, married his mother, Mary Alice Curry. Ernest Gooden's mother, Londi Curry, married Harry Gooden. Ernest took on the name of Gooden because his real father was a white man. Mary Alice Curry and Londi Curry were sisters, and their father's name was Brad Curry. Ernest told him that his mother had always told him that they were related to the Curry's in our family.

Before there was my mother Lula Bell Wyley Curry and her seven siblings, there were her mother Lula Hall Curry and her father Early Curry and before that was this lady named Chanie Hall. Chanie Hall appeared on the 1900 Census Report with her. My mother's oldest and the youngest outlived the other siblings as a boarder with the Remsen family. My grandma (my mother's mother) was at the age of fifteen. Chanie Curry Jones, my mother's oldest sister, was on this planet for one hundred and two years of age.

My ancestors were close and visited each other frequently, and that was awesome. Sometimes in the summer, when school was out, my mom packed our things and took us to the country, where there were no inside toilets and no running water, but regardless, I loved spending time with my grandparents. My grandpa would let me ride his horse and wagon to town, and that was so much fun. Saturday after work would be a time for us to go uptown and buy some things and meet other family members. That's why I loved the South and the Black world we lived in.

There was a lot of land to run and play. Lots of clean spring water from the creeks and wells. There were berries, cherries, pecan trees, oranges and lemon trees and others. God had put us on this planet and provided us with all the food and water to sustain life for those He chose to live on this planet.

To me, I think my mother's oldest sister, Chanie, was a little mean. However, we stayed at her house sometimes during the summer months. She had cold water and an outside toilet, whereas my other family had well-water and outdoor toilets. Last summer, when my mother sent my brother and me off to the country it was to stay with Aunt Chanie, that was a disaster because I was heading toward womanhood, and staying with her was a problem. The first night there, I turned the light on while sleeping, I never told her or anyone about the nightly visitor, the lady that stood at the foot of my bed except my mother. She would allow me to sleep with her sometimes, but for the most part I had to deal with the fear myself.

After my father died, a male spirit took over and maintained his presence throughout the 1950s, 1960s, 1970s, 1980s and 1990s before groups started to appear. My dreams were foreshadowing incidents that would happen outside my dream.

In introducing you to my ancestors I fell to include my Indian ancestors that prior to the beginning and ending of this book were unknown to me. Thank God for information. We must connect and continue to pray for God' s Grace. My goal is to learn as much about my new ancestors as well as the old.

Great-grandmother Chanie Hall

William and Mary Wiley

Chapter 2

GROWING UP BY THE RAILROAD TRACK

The little red house by the railroad was where the three of my parents' younger children were born, including me, their youngest. To sustain this house on a regular basis, we used coal and wood for heating and cooking. We used an icebox to keep the food fresh and for icy water. We huddled around the open fireplace in the front room to stay warm. Although we had a bathroom on the back porch, it was very cold, so we took baths in the kitchen, close to the log heater. The kitchen was hot enough to keep us warm throughout the house except when it was extremely cold. The red house is where my mom and dad lived together as a family unit and the most memories are.

The railroad track, built in the 1800s, was twelve feet from where the red house was located. It was a part of our daily lives as we walked up and down, across and around, to get where we had to go. We washed and boiled clothes in a big black iron pot close to the railroad, so they would be squeaky cleaned.

I didn't like the little red house by the railroad track, but from this place came my most memorable and happy moments.

Clothes were something that was of little importance when we were young. I remember just wearing my underwear and nothing at the top. You would think that there was no immoral behavior during that time, but it was. A male neighbor tried to encourage me to go with him up in the mountains so I could be with him but thank God my ancestors were not hearing it and made me get away from him. Never told this story to anyone, never my mother or dad.

My older sister, Katie, was my mother's first child to go off to college. My sister, Lula, got married just before graduating from high school. Her husband promised her she could continue and graduate while he worked.

After the wedding, he refused to work if she went to school. So, she quit school. Years later, she went back to school, got her high school diploma, and continued her education, becoming a registered nurse for the state of California. She worked in this position until her transition in 1996. As the only little girl in Noojin, Alley contributed to my being a tomboy. The older girls, like my sisters and their friends, did not play with me. Since my brother was only two years older, he would play with me, and so would my closest classmates. I could run, swim, do gymnastics and skate as well as any boy. If I could change things, I would not because of the love of family and friends and the times we shared. We did not have a television while living in the red house, only a radio and each of us huddling around the fireplace.

My daddy and the other men in the neighborhood would often go rabbit hunting. They would also kill hogs, cut them up, and share with others. Other groups want to go back to the good old days of slavery and killing, but what most Black people want to get back to safe communities, healthy food, love, and peace.

When I was two years old, my father went to World War II where he served for two years. The government would provide us with food. I remember being in the backyard where they distributed big hunks of cheese and other stuff that I cannot remember. I remember my dad writing my mother love letters, but not too long after his end of service, he remarried had two additional children, but left her to be with another woman and died while living with another woman.

My mother also remarried a man who had a job and had his own business and was also a preacher. He and my brother could not get along, which caused problems.

Because of my brother, my mother told her husband he had to leave her house, and she gave him until midnight into January first to pack his clothes and move out. I remember very well at midnight my brother hit the floor and then my sister and my mother hit the floor and since my stepfather was still there, they threw his things out the back door. My stepdad left, never to return. My older sister and I were the only ones to not participate in this throw out. After my mother and stepdad separated, my mother took me and my brother to government housing, where people lived called the 6th Street Projects. This was okay with me because I had my own room, a nice bathroom, bedroom, kitchen, and a heating system.

As I lay me down to sleep, I pray to the Lord my soul to keep and if I should die before I wake, I pray to the lord my soul to take. This was the prayer that my mother taught me and my siblings when we were children. My mother was a spiritual woman, strong in her faith and love of God. She was in her physical form a guiding force in my life and that force remains even in the spirit world.

At this point of my transformation, it was not relevant that this prayer was an imprinting to her thinking at the time that God represented something or someone other than someone who looked like her or me.

In my mother's house, you get up on Sunday morning and go to Sunday school and stay for church services. This was a ritual that we had to adhere to.

During the summer break, we also had to attend Bible school as well. This is what I call a church over kill. After graduating from high school at eighteen, I left my mother's house to marry the love of my life. I did not attend church regularly for twenty-seven years.

However, my mother taught me the power of prayer. Those teachings never waived during that period of my absence from the church. The power of prayer is at the forefront of my existence, and this is contributed to my prayerful mother and because I am who I am.

My mother worked hard to raise her children. She set an example and model for her children to follow. With my being the youngest, she stressed the importance of love and respect for us as well as others. Lula, as she was called, had many cliches and beliefs that probably had been passed down for many generations.

My mother taught us that one of the easiest things a person can do is to greet people with a simple good morning, hello, or good evening because it is not a harmful or evil act and does not work any ills against your neighbor.

Racism was alive and kicking. In my world, I was in a bubble and knew my place. However, my plan was to leave the South, never to return. How little did I know that my mother's teaching extended to self-awareness that would teach me survival skills, such as if you keep your hands closed, nothing will get in and nothing would get out. This comes from a woman who believed in giving, sharing, and helping others. Whatever job you have, do it well. If you shine shoes or sweep floors, do a good job. Don't beg for or borrow anything. If you start to bake a cake and discover you do not have a cup of sugar to bake the cake, just do not bake the cake.

Everything in my world was Black, as my parents, family, friends, communities with fish and barbecue stands—in my mind I was sitting on top of the world. It was a world where I was sheltered, protected, and loved by my parents. Of course, as a child, I considered them to be mean to me. Looking back, I realize everything they did was in my best interest.

On two separate occasions, my mother truly was upset with me. I had gone against her norms and needed a lesson to do good. The first lesson was when I stole her dime and when she asked me where it came from, I lied and said I had found it. She looked at the dime and saw that there was a hole in the dime, just like the one she wore around her neck. I paid for that. She whipped me good and taught me my first lesson: not to steal and never lie to her.

Lesson two was to have my chores done by the time she got off from work on Saturdays. My chores in my mother's house were to keep it clean. That meant I had to clean up my room, my brother's room, wash all his clothes plus my clothes, mop the floors, and keep the bathroom clean. My brother kept the yard mowed and would earn money cutting other people's grass on the weekends. He also went to the golf course to carry golf balls.

My mother's job was to work, pay the bills, cook, and provide food. Although her biggest meals were prepared on Saturday, she did not cook on Sundays. That was church time. One thing about my mom, once my task was done, I could go anywhere I wanted to if she knew where to put her hands on me from the time I left and the time for me to be home.

Lula cared about people she would visit, the sick and the dead at the funeral homes. Shortly after Christmas 1953, my mother took me with her to see my dad, who was seriously ill. I got in the bed next to my dad because I was tired and sleepy. That past Christmas he gave my brother and all the boys bicycles but didn't get me one and I didn't like that. He promised to get me one next Christmas. What he did get me for my present was a beautiful blue two-piece sweater set.

That same night, my dad started coughing. It woke me up, and I knew he was sick. Shortly after that, he passed at the young age of thirty-five years old. God took my dad in August, and I met Bobby in September the same year, but he sent me Bobby, my husband, shortly after that when I was in the seventh grade. How strange that the same year my daddy transitioned, the love of my life appeared in my life. The spirit of the man started to chase me in my dreams.

I wasn't the child that stayed out of school. Meaning, I didn't play hooky because my mother was very strict. However, I stayed home one day and just stayed in bed and slept. This was a mistake because in my sleep, a man began to chase me, causing me to wake up hollering and very frightened. From that day on, the man took over chasing me and the woman went away. Thinking about who the man was, I would say now it was my dad. Even though he was in the spirit world, he continued to protect me. No one I talked to could explain what was going on.

I was walking down the stairs at school one day and some guy came up the stairs to the right of me and slapped me in the face. I found out later that he had made a bet with his friend that he would slap me.

Bobby approached me after that and asked for my number even though I could not date until sixteen years of age. After Bobby had slapped me, he disappeared, and I continued going to school, participating in sports, running track, and playing the clarinet. There were four other young men who were interested in me by their actions. A young man who lived about five miles away in Attalla, who would go down in 6th Street Projects, looking for girls. This person was about six feet tall, and I did not like him. My mother eventually ran him away. Another one came to my house and bought me a watch; he wanted my mother's approval to date me, but she told him don't come back into her house anymore. This other young man was older and more experience and had served in the US Navy, so I had to be strong because he did not respond to the answer no. This one escaped my mother, and he was the one she should have been worried about. He wanted to marry me after graduation. I was not there yet, but I was headed toward sixteen and I would have my mother's permission to date.

As the years went by, Bobby's family moved into the projects and a couple of years later, I found out that Bobby had gone into the military. Never saw him anymore until I was sixteen and had dated one of his close friends.

Sam Cook released his famous record "Only Sixteen" in 1959 and the Crests released their hit song, "Sixteen Candles." I was enjoying being sixteen with these beautiful hit songs playing all the time. I was not interested in anyone at the time he entered back into my life. He loved the records also and purchased the songs for me.

The railroad behind the house.

Chapter 3

IT'S MY TIME TO DATE

My mother was always running the boys away from our home, as usual, by telling them not to come back anymore. I later found out that my brother would put her up to sending boys away also, by telling my mother to send them away because he felt that if he were home, they should be home as well. If we went to the country to go to the hole in the wall, he would get my aunt to take me home because he really didn't want me dancing with anyone. My mother, on the other hand, didn't mind the boys there if they maintained a respectable distance. But that was before I turned sixteen. If they kept their distance, my mother would not be that bad because it was not like we were dating, but things would be different because I was now sixteen years old, and she had approved that I could date at that age. Sixteen years old was also the ongoing age for all girls to date during this time.

The fourth guy that really liked me for me and not for sex was my very first date. He was a tall, handsome nice guy who was also Bobby's friend. After Bobby and I really became a couple, his friend, who would call me periodically, backed away from calling me. In doing so, he gave me information on knowing how far to go with a boy. He gave me good advice, and I adhered to it because I trusted him.

He picked me up from my home and we walked to the movies. We didn't have cars, so we walked everywhere. Even if I had a car, I could not drive because my mother had not taught me how to drive. Although my mother could drive and had her own car, repairs were costly.

My mother worked in a laundry, pressing clothes all day long. She worked eight hours, six days a week, and half days on Saturday with no breaks to rest and low wages. The demanding work and standing on her feet six days a week broke her down, making it difficult to work.

The good thing about working in the laundry is that my brother's clothes were taken care of. My mother took all his clothes for washing and pressing but didn't take any of my things. Before I graduated from high school, my mother got her another job working in a very upscale hotel where Black people were not allowed hotel services.

I went to the carnival one night and up comes Bobby and my friend together. It was rumored that they were a couple, along with five other girls. Older guys were beginning to talk to me and that was a good thing, so I was doing okay.

One night I was walking home from my sister's house when Bobby walked up to me and asked me for a date to the movies. I said yes. My mother never knew about it because it was her club night, and she would be late coming home. In the theater, Bobby sat on my right side and held my arm up throughout the movie. My arm was so tired.

After the movie date, Bobby returned to his military base and started to send me letters. In examining the mail, my mother discovered that I had received mail from a man that she did not know. My mother had not seen Bobby, but she knew one of his brothers would come and talk to me in our backyard from time to time.

She was pleased that he was one of the Chancellor boys because they were all nice young men. Bobby's three-year term of duty was coming up and he would be ending his tour of duty with the United States Army. In his first letter, he asked me to be his girlfriend and, of course, I said yes. At the time, I did not think about my girlfriend, or other girls that he had dated or wanted to date.

I called my girlfriend because she and I would often go to the skating rink and movies together. We were also in the school band, and both played second clarinet. One day she told me she liked a boy back then there were good girls and there were bad girls, and this boy was not the type a good girl would date. At the same time, she liked another boy. This was the reason I was surprised she went around telling the whole neighborhood that I had stolen her boyfriend.

Bobby and I both fell head over heels in love with each other. The love we shared lasted through our divorce. He promised to always take care of me even if we did not stay together, and he did.

Our second date was formidable. That led to wanting to be with just each other. He wanted to be with me only and I wanted to be with him only. My mother told me the neighbor three apartments down from us was talking about me and Bobby and that I was going to get pregnant. I told my mother the neighbor had better watch her own daughter because I was not doing anything.

She did not know that her daughter was playing hooky from school while she was at work. Her daughter was allowing this older boy to come into her home when she was alone and eventually got pregnant.

One Sunday night my mother told Bobby to leave her house and not to come back anymore. In fact, she told him never to speak to me anyone. This devastated me because we loved each other. Later that week, I saw him at the softball game, and he walked up to me, and we made another date and agreed that we would end our date at 10:00 p.m. so my mother would not get angry again.

Later, I heard that Bobby had bought me an engagement ring, which did not surprise me because, at this point, we were ready to live together. I now wonder why I thought that at that age I should be married.

On Christmas night, Bobby proposed to me without recognizing my mother for her blessing or approval at all. He was ready to take me off into the sunset and forever more, but things were not that easy. Along with the engagement came orders for no more tight skirts or nail polish. I could not even get my ears pierced.

Bobby took me to my senior prom, and that was nice. He took me up there and stayed outside to take me home. We would get to know each other better, but after we became engaged, we would have arguments regularly, and break up every week. This was a sign that we were not ready or equipped for married life.

One Friday I was walking my friend home and my friend asked, "Is that Bobby up there?" and I said, "Yes." They were walking with their arms around each other, and their heads bent over touching each other. As I approached them, I asked him where he was going and he said, "With you." He took me home and, of course, I gave him back his ring only to put it back week after week.

We wanted to get married, so we planned a date and time to get married.

We went across the state line into Georgia because I was underage. On the same morning that we planned to get married, my mother instructed me to go stay with my sister who was in labor. My sister was holding on as the baby began to exit from the womb. I was so frightened that I ran downstairs and to my sister's house to help.

During this time, we all stayed in the projects and lived close to each other. I remember the doctor getting there as her beautiful baby girl, Janet, came onto this planet. My sister, who had children of her own, knew what to do until the doctor arrived. Our plans to get married were put on hold by nature, and we had nothing to do with it.

We were disappointed that our plans to get married did not happen. My mother, when I told her of my plans to get married, pleaded with me and made me promise her we would not get married before graduation and I had received my high school diploma.

Because Bobby could not secure a job there in our hometown, he went to Ohio, hopefully to get a job. I really didn't want him to leave, but I wished him well. After my high school graduation, I got a job washing dishes at the Catholic Hospital where my older sister worked. Bobby returned home because he could not find a job, so he said that he didn't want me to be there without him.

Once again, Bobby signed up for another tour of duty with the US Army because there was no income for him. Because he was leaving, we once again planned to get married since I was out of high school. We put everything in order like blood tests and application to get married.

This time, it was his family that intervened in us getting married. They felt since he had to leave me, to report back to duty, it would not be good for us to get married. It appears we would never get married. This was hurtful but did not stop my plans to leave Gadsden and venture out on my own.

My mother, thank God, raised me to move into the world with proper skills and common sense. Walking to my job on the first day, I saw a cute little white luggage to pack my clothes in. I didn't have the money to pay up front for the luggage, so I put it on a layaway plan until my next payday and I paid for it.

This was during the great migration to different cities for different jobs like Detroit and New York. For poor girls, that also included my classmates who couldn't afford college, so they went to New York as house maids. I was eighteen years old and grown and could do what I wanted to do.

At the time, Bobby and I started to date the few friends I had put on the back burner. Bobby took the first and top position in my life, allowing space for others.

Because Bobby and I made a lovely couple, there were differences. He was more reserved, and I was outspoken, causing us to clash often. He put me on a pedestal where I needed to be and kept me there until he transitioned from where he came from.

Getting married was the proper thing to do since we truly loved each other.

We were not engaged in sexual activities but did a little flirting on the front porch. We took his mother's and aunt's advice about us waiting to get married until he was settled. The only difference was that I was not going to continue to wait and gave him the only ultimatum that I had ever given anyone and the only one that I had given to this date. I was anxious to get married, start a family, and live happily ever after. The best thing in the world for him to do was to send for me because I would not have given birth to our lovely children.

Chapter 4

PACKING MY BAGS AND
LEAVING HOME

Stationed in Virginia, Bobby didn't know what to do about us, so I informed him what I was going to do. I was heading to New York to get a maid's job. He told me to wait until he could send me money to get a train and come to Virginia.

Once, while in the school band, I traveled to Nashville, Tennessee to participate in a musical competition. That was exciting, but this time I was on my own and was going to get married and have babies. There was love for each other and I trusted him to take care of my well-being. My mother trusted him also to allow me to go that far to get married. His family wished me well after Bobby informed them, I would be heading to Virginia to become his wife.

The first night there, we stayed in a hotel room because the rental would not be ready until the next day. Bobby had secured a rental room in a rooming house in Newport News, Virginia, sharing the bathroom and kitchen.

Bobby and I had a romantic dinner that night while listening to "Georgia on My Mind" by Ray Charles, which was one of the top songs of that era and our love song. Even though we had left home, he still respected my wishes of being married before engaging in sex.

In all our planning, we failed to inquire about the legal age to marry in the state of Virginia.

We went to the courthouse to marry, where we were told the legal age in Virginia was twenty-one years of age and I was just eight years old. I had to have a certified signature from my mother, granting us her permission to get married. At the age of eighteen, I became a wife and left my mother's house for my husband's house to be controlled and told what I could and couldn't do.

Soon after we got married, I became pregnant and the discomfort and throwing up sent me home to my mother.

The birth of my firstborn and the beautiful trailer that my husband had rented for us made me happy. We lived in a trailer court with other military families. I returned to be with my husband, which made me happy, but then began noticing there was something about me that caused me to question who I was.

One Sunday morning I was sleeping and heard the telephone ringing. It was my mother slumped over in a chair saying she was dying. "Not now, but I am dying," she said. It concerned me to where I went to Alabama to see her but didn't tell her why. This was the first time I had spoken or written about this to anyone.

As I headed back to Alabama amid the Civil Rights Movement, a lot of things were going on. The colored signs posted in the bathrooms when I left had all been removed. Physically seeing my mother was okay. I returned home, storing this in my mind, regretting the day my mom would leave me.

The things that were happening to me I couldn't explain. They were scary, although someone gave me a name for the man that woke me up in my dream, chasing me, calling them nightmares. And later, I was told they were my ancestors.

We moved from the trailer court to Williamsburg, Virginia, to an apartment not too far from the base. As soon as we had bought new furniture, Bobby came home with orders to move to another military base outside of Washington, DC. This was frustrating, especially when it was very difficult to secure an apartment for the three of us within proximity of the base. We had no choice but to move into the big District of Columbia to find a place to live. It was also hard to get an apartment if you had children. We were lucky to find a room sharing the bathroom, kitchen, and a cat

The family we lived with were very nice, but the distance and the only one auto made it difficult for Bobby to commute from the base to home every night because he would have to double back to work when needed. Bobby's tour of duty was ending, and he decided not to reenlist. We returned to Alabama, although I didn't want to. I had to follow my husband.

I could not take care of myself and our child. We lived with Bobby's mother because she had more room. That wasn't a good idea because we began to argue. I left his mother's house and went back to Virginia, but got as far as Nashville, Tennessee. Bobby's mother answered the phone and told him not to put any long-distance charges on her phone so we couldn't talk for long. After that call, I returned to Alabama and stayed with my mother.

The girl that Bobby was walking home with that night when we came into the picture again. I was told that they were seen all hugged up leaving the Skyline together. It looked like my marriage was headed to be over because I didn't want people calling me, telling me what my husband was doing. I packed my suitcase and my daughter, and we left for Los Angeles, California. I never called to tell him I was leaving or who I would be staying with. I loved him, but I was not going to hang around listening to gossip about him and some other woman. If he wanted me, he would have to come and get me.

The most beautiful thing about California was the palm trees as the Greyhound bus cruised down the road with me and my daughter, Tammy. I was excited to be leaving the South to have a better life for my child. Since my husband was having fun, I had no intention of having any more babies.

It took about two days after I left before Bobby called my mother inquiring as to the whereabouts of his wife and daughter. My mother told him we were in California. My mother gave him my address so he could write to me. He, of course, was very upset that I didn't tell him before heading to California. He was upset and angry and I believe that he never got over it or forgave me for leaving.

Shortly after, Bobby sent me a letter informing me that he had reenlisted in the military and would leave Alabama to begin his tour of duty in Frankfurt, Germany. He wanted me and our daughter to join him as a family. We agreed we would leave Los Angeles and return to Alabama and start the process. Ft. McClellan US Military Base is where my daughter was born and where our immunizations protected us from different diseases when entering another country.

While living in Los Angeles, I found a job in a hamburger/hot dog stand, but it was not to pay for my room and buy food for my daughter. We all stayed in a hotel that rented out extended living, however it wasn't the best, but it was affordable. My uncle Houston and my brother took care of my daughter and me during our stay in Los Angeles. Bobby, as soon as he had money coming in, he also sent us money. We decided to return to Alabama and began the process of joining Bobby in Germany

I stayed with my sister, Lula Mae, until I left to be with my husband in Frankfurt, Germany. Just before I left, my sister gave birth to her last baby girl, Tina. Lula was soon to relocate to Los Angeles to be with her husband, who had relocated there just before we left California, returning to Alabama.

I didn't get a chance to spend time with any of my friends or family while I was once again in my hometown. I was now a married woman with a child and really didn't have time. Although the gossip that I took about my best friend's boyfriend was still circling, other than that my family was intact and would be coming together soon.

When it was time for our departure, we left the airport on a plane about the size of a helicopter, and I was scared. We transferred from this plane in South Carolina onto a larger plane that was more durable for the long flight ahead. We left at midnight, arriving that next morning at daybreak. I woke up when the pilot announced we were heading over to Paris.

Bobby secured us a very nice apartment in a rooming house type of environment temporarily because neither one of us wanted to share a bathroom with the others. Another military family also lived in the rooming house with us a soldier, his wife, and son, the wife, was a nice person and unique to me because she would get up in the morning, putting on makeup lipstick, face power, and eye makeup whereas I never put any lipstick on unless I was leaving the house. We also were renting from a landlord who didn't like Americans and the United States. All she talked about was that Russia would someday take down the US.

We were already in a war with Vietnam and my husband, an MP, had to guard the wall that separated the East from West Germany. He also could be sent to Vietnam at any time. I was also glad to move to our more permanent residence.

All that rhetoric cleared up when we moved into our more permanent residence. Bobby secured a permanent place for us from one of the German interpreters who worked on the Army base—a one-bedroom, kitchen, bathroom, dayroom, and a balcony. Finks, the interpreter landlord, had living quarters downstairs with his wife and daughter, a very nice family. The daughter was fixated on my daughter. I had to watch her when in the presence of my daughter because she would take others could see her hair and color. I think it was the first time she had seen a Black child before and was fascinated by her.

Germany is a beautiful country. It didn't take me long to learn my way around the beautiful countryside, looking at the large flock of sheep grazing in the grass. Bobby taught me how to drive a stick shift so that we could purchase a Volkswagen. I learned to speak a little German to do the things I wanted to do. While enjoying myself, God gave me another pregnancy. This pregnancy was not an easy one. I was sick all the time, throwing up every time I got into an automobile.

My false labor was upon me, so I stayed in the hospital for three days before they sent me home. My doctor told me to walk around because that would move the baby down. After arriving home and cooking our favorite breakfast egg and cheese omelet and hot links the pains had become more regular and painful. However, I didn't want to go back into the hospital, so I ignored them until they got so sharp, I had to go. Bobby took me to the branch clinic, and from there they sent me in an ambulance to the 97th General Hospital in Frankfurt, Germany, where my second daughter was born on a hospital gurney while being transported through the hallway to the delivery room.

There was nothing I could remember or had documented as a blizzard dream while sleeping in the bed with my husband except for my mother calling me to tell me she was dying, as documented in an earlier chapter. Maybe this spirit felt that I was okay and that he didn't have to show up every night and ward off others who wished me harm.

It was also good to have family members to visit while in Germany. Bobby's older brother, Willie Joe, lived on the other side of the Nile River, the longest river in the world. It was exciting crossing over on a boat a river that crosses through the countries of Africa.

Bobby's brother met and fell in love with a beautiful German girl. Rosa was one of the nicest people that I had ever met. She was honest, sincere, and straightforward in so many ways. She transitioned and I know she is in a good place.

I was compelled to take a ride on the train one day to visit Bobby while he was away training. I had ridden trains many times before, but nothing like this. It was like we were there in a flash. Bobby had secured a nice room for the four of us. I must say the room was the nicest that I had stayed in. The room had hardwood floors, and everything was spotless.

After waking up the next morning, I saw what it was like outside, and to my surprise, when I opened the door, I saw the most beautiful mountain, which appeared to be approximately twelve feet from the door. Later I was told that we were in Oberammergau in the Bavarian Village. This was where the European passion for Christ is acted out every ten years.

It was difficult for us to get along. No matter how much we loved each other, we just couldn't seem to make it work. We were always arguing, and I was always throwing things at him. It is hard now to believe that the young me would throw things at a big, strong man like my husband, but I did. I came back to the US to find a job and take care of myself and my two children.

Chapter 5

COMING INTO MY OWN

On my second travel to Los Angeles, God increased my contribution to the Universe with another beautiful daughter. My trip this time was more permanent, and I had saved money to sustain us financially. My sister and her children had now joined her husband; also, my uncle's family had now joined him. It seems like my mother's lineage had all except for Katie, my older sister, had migrated to California. My mother came to visit on a few occasions.

On my first night in L.A., I stayed with my sister. Then we moved into our apartment on 110th Street and Normandie. The landlord was a nice lady. What I remember most about her is that she taught me how to write a check using a checkbook, which was a new experience for me. However, I was still in my early twenties with two children and had never been alone before, but capable of taking care of myself.

Los Angeles was a booming city, a working city with an abundance of jobs, including government positions with rewarding benefits that would maintain a decent lifestyle when you reached retirement status.

Arriving in Los Angeles, we stayed with my sister, who had one daughter, and was being taken care of by my uncle and brother financially, while I lived in an extended hotel environment. This time, I had my own apartment and some money to sustain our financial needs.

Again, my husband and I made up and his tour of duty was ending in a few months, and he wanted to come to California where we were and try to make our marriage work, I agreed because I wanted the same thing, knowing fully that I would always love him regardless of if we stayed together or not.

Knowing it was going to be a problem, I put my efforts into getting me a job before he arrived because he had a problem with me working on a job. I took tests for jobs and was hired at McDougal's Aircraft. On the day I was to report working I didn't have anyone to keep my children. It was a failed opportunity to have a good income to help with the household.

Bobby had the car shipped to New York, where he picked it up and drove it to L.A. When it comes to directions, you can't beat him because he was very good at it. He taught me how to do road travel across the country by counting miles and assessing the length of time from city to city and state to state.

My uncle helped my husband get a job by asking his boss to take him aboard. A good indication: it's not always what you know, but who you know. Bobby worked there one week before the US Postal Service called him for orientation. He had taken the test and if he passed the orientation, he would be hired. In addition, he had to pass his scheme that involved getting to know all the streets in Los Angeles. He had to distribute one hundred cards and was only allowed to miss five cards to pass at 95% correct.

Bobby didn't care that much for distributing mail because all his skills fell into law enforcement, whereas he served as a Military Policeman during his entire military service.

God saw fit to allow me to bring another child into the world. We were excited about having a son. My mother came to visit us to help with the baby. This was her first time traveling so far from her home. Bobby didn't care that much for my mother because of how she treated him when we were dating, although he was always cordial.

As the children started to grow, I wanted to go back to school, so I went to register for Southwest Junior

College to take some classes. The process was long, with wrap-around lines. I got home to find my husband had packed his clothes and left his wife and three children. He eventually came home. It was clear he didn't want me to work and didn't want me to go to school.

Being stubborn, I went to work at Sears department store as a cashier during the holidays. I came home from work and my baby son was screaming and looked to have been crying for a long time. I quit and promised myself to wait until my son was a little older.

When my frequency level began to elevate my dreams began to come to fruition, whether it was something that would happen, something or someone I would see. I would see it in my dreams before it happened. One night I went to check on my children who were sleeping in one bedroom. As I headed into the room, I saw a shadow that was coming back into the bedroom. I picked up an object to protect my family. Bobby was on the swing shift and wouldn't be home until after midnight, so I had to protect my little ones.

In my mind, there was a man in the house, but thanks to God, there was nobody but a shadow who was my uncle who died a few days after seeing the shadow. This was in 1969.

You can't predict or change God's plans that have been laid out for you. Once again, God gave me another girl to take her position as the baby of the family. Before she was born, we bought a house with a large back and front yard with a large apricot and lemon tree. The back yard and the front yard were large enough for our children to run and play.

My baby girl was three months old when my husband and I separated, but I would like to think we tried and did the best we could but the paths we took were the ones for us and we were prompted into those directions at the will of God.

When I first became pregnant, I took the written test issued by the Post Office to determine at the minimum that individuals could meet the skills as required by the Post Office. However, when they called me for a medical, I disclosed I was pregnant and asked to be placed on the back of the waiting list. After the birth of our daughter, I was placed back on the waiting list to be called for a physical.

Three months after the birth of our daughter, I was hired by the Post Office. But I had a scheme that I had to qualify to maintain my job. I was assigned as a distribution clerk, whereas I had to learn and distribute mail to all cities in the state of California. I was given all the cities but to pass I could not miss but five within 5 minutes.

Having a job was what I wanted to acquire the things I wanted and live the lifestyle that I wanted. My first check I went to a department store and bought a washing machine. I couldn't work and go to the washhouse. I took it upon myself, without discussing it with my husband. I was still in my twenties with four children, our own home, and an excellent job, but a husband who didn't feel loved, wanted, or needed. The responsibilities were too much for the both of us, but he was the one who walked.

There is a reason for everything, and it is done for a purpose. We have been put here for a purpose. God will remove all things to clear the path for you to allow you to fulfill that job that He wants you to do. It has been a long road and process for me to get to this understanding, and as I have so often asked myself, "Who am I?" Who was I to be so important that the ancestors would come gather to protect me?

My mother has never left me. Her spirit surrounds me and consoles me when I am in distress and protects me when I am in harm's way. On many occasions, my mother and my dad had to show up and protect me. I have had a rental car to break, a flat tire, and keys locked in the auto.

When I was younger, we traveled all over the place. First Route 66 and then I-40 and Interstate 10. Route 66 was the most famous interstate to travel on at that time and for some reason I-40 was the one to travel on. We were a family who took road trips during my vacation time. Even when my husband and I divorced, we still took road trips with the children. We went to the World Fair, and I remember when we were returning, it was announced that President Nixon had resigned from office. During this time, I could have cared less about who was president because I was a single mom with four children, working very hard trying to survive.

The last road trip I took by myself was a little scary. I had to drive a large, big wheeler from Alabama to California. I had rented a moving truck but didn't realize how long it really was. I almost fainted when I saw the length of this big truck. The truck was needed to move my furniture from my house to storage. After the movers loaded the truck, I went to the bank, misjudging the clearance bar at the drive-thru for the drive-up teller; the truck knocked the entire bar down to the ground.

The bank was closing, so I had to go back the next morning to report the damage. After reporting the damage and notifying my insurance company, I left to visit my aunt who was one hundred and one years old. I was so glad I did because that was the last time, I saw her alive.

Chapter 6

FOLLOWING MY DREAMS

After Bobby left, I couldn't cry because I had four small children to take care of and didn't have the time.

He said he would always take care of me, and he did. He would come over the night before trash day and set the trash out until my son took over the job.

I wouldn't be telling the truth if I said I didn't love my husband because I loved him very much. God, knowing what was ahead for me, had set the path for me to have a reasonably good job with benefits before he removed him from the home. There were lessons for me to learn. After I left my mother, who took care of me until my husband, I was going to have a tough time, but I would survive. I had to learn how to take care of myself.

I had no idea what my job was going to be like. I was hired as a clerk and my task was to distribute mail as letters, parcels large and small. The Post Office is multi-faceted, with many different tasks involved daily. This was where my mother's teachings came into play— whatever job you do, work hard—and this is what I did. I selected my friends carefully as my mother taught me and they had to have a very high work ethic, otherwise they could not hang around me.

Distribution of mail was exactly what I did. I was always good with my hands, so I could work very fast. I made myself a box case to practice my scheme, knowing that I only had a short time to solidify my position as a clerk.

I immediately met friends that did the same things that I like to do, playing bid whist. In my marriage, I only had my husband's friends and when he left, so did they.

The first thing I did was get my ears pierced, remove my bra, and put some hoops in my ears. I also bought a pair of jeans and a miniskirt, as I was getting into my own and no one told me what to wear and who my friends should be.

Caring for four children as a single parent was not easy. We worked out together each of our parenting roles to better meet the needs of our children. Since I was working and receiving a decent wage, I didn't ask him what I could have received, but what I felt was reasonable. He agreed. If I needed more money or anything, he was there. He bought me a house on his GI Bill because I couldn't qualify. When he was sick and transitioning, all our children came there in the same house to care for him as he prepared to leave the physical world.

Distributing mail wasn't my goal, and I had to find me something else to do. Jobs were available, but I didn't have the college course classes I needed to meet the job requirements.

It was now time for me to set my goals and make another attempt to continue my education. To do this, I enrolled at the nearby junior college to pursue a major in Business Administration. I would later transfer to a university to achieve a bachelor's degree. However, the interplays of the best laid plans are sometimes unreachable.

One of my dreams, when growing up, was to join the military. For me that was exciting. We lived about twenty-eight miles from Fort McClellan Air Force Base in Anniston, Alabama. They would send a bus for girls to go onto the base to socialize with the GIs. My mother wouldn't allow me to go because I was too young. Maybe the contributing factor for my joining the Army Reserve was because of the social nature and lots of men and the need to get away from the breakup of my marriage. Although I didn't date until my divorce was settled, to show proper respect to my fifteen-year marriage.

I was with some friends the last day and the closing of Ft. McArthur in Long Beach, California. All the drinks were reduced or free in celebration of the closing. I was also celebrating that I had received my orders to soon leave for basic training at Ft. Jackson, South Carolina.

Leaving my children to go into the military wasn't a thought-out plan, but it was something I had to do on my path to learning who I was. I also picked up skills and discipline that prepared me to endure some of the most difficult periods of my life. My first time at basic training, I was met by people hollering, "Get to the ground!" I asked myself, "Is this what I left my children for?" In addition, I had to place the custody of my children under the care of my mother. My specialty in the military was Finance. The courses that I had taken, like accounting and finance, prepared me for my MOS.

Things were so different, and I had to learn lessons upon lessons to survive the many experiences placed upon me. There was a welcoming social activity on the first day of basic training, where women and men came together. We talked and danced.

After that night, it was all rough and tough running, exercising, walking and learning. I met a guy, and we moved to a more private part of the building. He wanted to talk to me and to kiss and, to my surprise, I did as well. In basic training I found myself surrounded by much younger women doing foolish things. Two girls slipped out of the barracks one night thinking that they wouldn't get caught, but they did. The women were natural born snitches, telling no matter what you did. I loved being by myself, so I would take a shower in the early morning while the other girls were sleeping. Of course, I was told on, resulting in the restriction of early morning showers.

One day, the drill sergeant instructed us to go outside to play softball, which was something I was never good at; I couldn't hit the ball or catch it. I don't remember being good at basketball either.

My drill sergeant was a nice man, but we worked with all drill sergeants, depending on the assignment. I couldn't believe he just sent us out in the rain to play ball.

I started complaining because I didn't want to get wet, however it was fun and turned out to be one of my memorable days, as playing baseball in the rain was a memorable occasion. The worst was KP and injuries.

The KP duties were in the kitchen and that entailed everything involved, starting at three o'clock in the morning to prepare breakfast. Cleaning the house was my chore at home, so I knew how to mop a floor, but each time I completed the mopping, he would say, "Go over the floor. It isn't clean." This went on for several mopping before I was told that the floor was clean.

After my duty ended, I returned to my job and school. Attending school wasn't easy. I still had to go home, cook, and take care of my children. I would take my young daughter with me to my classes on many occasions. On the day of graduation, I was too tired to pick up my diploma. However, I requested to have it mailed to my residence.

After I received my degree, majoring in Business Administration and a minor in Management, I submitted my request for a training position as a US Postal Supervisor.

My course classes in management had prepared me for this position. John, I will call him the superintendent, denied my request. I immediately sent him my response with the question: Why? While working on my assignment, I heard the manager was looking for me. Because I had improper footwear on, I ran into the bathroom to hide my shoes with my toes open. As I exited the restroom, he wanted me to walk with him. As we walked, he was asking a lot of questions. I did not know that he was interviewing me.

He informed me he was considering another person as well. We lingered at the last area we walked, and this is where he told me to take off Saturday, Sunday, and report back Monday morning to the same area, to General Supervisor Mary Jackson at 7:00 a.m. Monday morning.

I must say that Mary was God sent. Her personality and mind clicked. This doesn't happen often for me because I am a follower only if you are going somewhere with a purpose. I can't waste my time by going up and down the street and around the corner. She took me under her wings, so to speak, and mentored me. When we were going under reconstruction at the Post Office, we all lost our jobs and did not know if we would be rehired. Mary came to me saying, "I do not know if anyone else will get a job, but you will." She always had my back.

Mary taught me all the ins and outs of processing mail. When you are sleeping, someone is wide awake working hard to ensure that you get your mail in a timely manner. There are people that are critical of the US Postal Service without merit. As compared to the other delivery services, the Post Office is the best.

From the time your mail is submitted to the box, it must be processed before it is delivered to you. The Processing Supervisor ensures that the mail is properly processed. After the mail is processed, it goes to the station to be prepared by the person that delivers your mail. These supervisors are the ones on the customer services side to ensure your deliveries.

After my promotion to Supervisor of Mail Processing, I was assigned a night job from 10:00 pm to 7:00 am, a shift that I did not like. Although I maintained high work ethics in my performance, the night shift was not for me. Eventually I was assigned a day job—7:00 am 3:30 pm. My tour of duty at the USPS ended in April 2000.

It confirmed that if I had not followed my instincts

to accept the job as a postal employee, my life may not have been so fruitful and rewarding. Being a Black woman from the South, I was looking for security. My mother was proud of her children. All her insisting that we graduate from high school paid off. Her first born was a college graduate. Her second born was a registered nurse. The third born was a high school graduate and the fourth born was a college graduate and a professional paralegal (legal assistant).

I went back to church with a co-worker who told me the service was from a Black perspective and was sure I would love it. The following Sunday after speaking to him, I went to the church and was surprised to see the blackness with a Black Jesus above the altar, and to hear the amazing choir, nothing that I had ever heard before.

For the next five years, I never missed a Sunday. The church was my life. My daughter, who has an unbreakable faith as a Catholic, was finishing her bachelor's degree and my youngest daughter joined me and we worked hard in the church. I served the community by starting a Mentoring Ministry that partnered with the Big Sisters. Our ministry would host events to recruit ladies to mentor so they could prosper in life, being the best person, they could be. The girls were recruited from the nearby junior high school, perhaps considered at-risk girls. We sold coffee and donuts every Sunday before and after the traditional and gospel masses to sponsor our programs. My daughter took Catholic Teaching of the Catholic Faith. My sponsor was responsible for enlightening and assisting me and answering any questions about what, how, and why they do things.

St. Brigid, a big church of Black congregants, offered me this spiritual feeding that I needed in my life. God placed people in my life to guide and bring me into preparedness and awareness of where I needed to be. We, as Black people, are spiritual and our music is uplifting. Babies come into the world with rhythm. It's not bragging, it's a fact. No babies are like ours. They have studied them and have come up with ways to lead them into drugs as consumers and or dealers. If you think that there is not a well-thought plan to lead in the self-destruction of our young, Black men, carefully think about it and ask who benefited the most from drugs in our community and who suffered the most from the outbreak of crack cocaine.

All you had to do was walk down the streets and see the devastation. I was a bid whist player during the 1970s and 1980s and would go anywhere to play cards. One night I ended up in the Jordan Down Projects, looking for my friend's house to play cards. I quickly learned there were places you did not go to at night by yourself. During that time there, my dream of having a husband who loved me and would stay with me always crumpled, so I pursued another one of my dreams and that was to have fun. I was worn out from working and taking care of my family with never enough money. I would sometimes get off from work at midnight and go to a card party and stay up all night and go home. For some reason I couldn't hold alcohol; one tablespoon would make me woozy. On the night of my senior prom, we went to a club in Anniston down the road from my hometown for our afterparty. I drank a little, but I was in safe hands because I was with my husband-to-be and my big brother; they knew I was off limits and to tread carefully.

My body resisted alcohol made me ill, cigarettes that made me cough I wanted to maintain good health and God was continually keeping me on the right track of what to consume and what not to consume including medicines and animal meat The culture of the world in which we live in is one of medication overdose, side effects, cancer radiation, chemo, surgical removal of body limbs, and diabetes. My mother was the doctor for her children. Whatever she gave me made me feel better, and at the same time healed my body.

With my children, I was comfortable with doctors who usually provided medication. Penicillin was the antibiotics that was the medicine to give when my children had earache, sore throat, or something of that nature. Where did all the medicine come from with all its side effects?

Now we are on a reverse path from pharmaceuticals to herbals to treat most diseases. There is a development of holistic doctors providing alternative treatments as opposed to pharmaceuticals and the harsh side effects. Our bodies are temples of God and should be treated as so.

Chapter 7

THE EVOLUTION OF MY MIND

As the body evolves, we become more intuitive as the mind leads us to a higher level of thinking while filtering information, showing things we wouldn't ordinarily see. I am still evolving and changing, even though the earth is very toxic. "Who am I"

The changing and advancement of the realization of who you are and how you got here in this time in space is like the caterpillar who has reached a certain frequency and evolves into this beautiful, colorful butterfly. Would it be okay to say that when man, in his efforts for a quicker way to get something done and in doing so is destroying the planet earth, is on a frequency too close to God? Technology, machines, chemicals, and cell phones come with a need but with a price, as toxic air, dirty water, hybrid food and animal meat limit your ability to gain access to these gifts.

I would say that we all don't arrive at the frequency at the same time some people call this awareness Woke or conscious. This awareness taps you into the third eye and your special gifts god has bestowed upon you.

The beauty of nature is that it provides us with all that we need to survive. We are supposed to live in harmony with other species on this planet and not eat them. My mother kept goldfish in water bowls throughout the house. It was my job to keep the bowls clean. My mother loved animals, although she kept cats but no dogs. A spiritual person is in tune with nature and other species of the earth and understands the earth is alive and should be maintained free of toxic waste.

My teaching into the Catholic faith brought forth for the first time an explanation of what I was going through, beginning with the lady who stood by my bed. To be accepted into the faith of Catholicism, I had to complete my teaching of the faith. After the teaching, I was baptized in the name of the Father, Son, and the Holy Spirit. My daughter, Renate, and I shared the same ceremony and were baptized together. Although my four children received Catholic school education, only one remains in the church.

After the LA rebellion, the community came together, desiring an outlet to vent their outrage and utter disgust of the blatant abuse as perpetrated on a citizen. Two hosts of a radio show allowed people to vent and discuss daily issues from 4:00 a.m. to 6:00 a.m. Monday through Friday also the community gathering continued every Friday night. It was a privilege and honor to hear the many people that shared and informed us of all the greatness of our people.

What an honor to hear the teachings of our great scholars talk about the seven circuits of the brain. It was a privilege all day at workshops to hear some of the brightest minds who spoke about Christianity and Environmental Racism.

Through all this time, my understanding shifted. I began wondering, why are we still talking about Mark, Luke, and John when my people were struggling and gang banging, and no one seems to care? Although I was highly active in the church—sitting on the Parish Council, giving communion to the sick and other tasks in the church—the gathering of the Black church was always in the forefront. God was talking to me, and I was coming into myself. I now know that God has provided us with the gifts of the Holy Spirit.

On October 30, 2000, for the first time, I bought a journal. I have been under the belief that what you don't want people to know, don't put it in writing. For years, the unusual things that happened and still happen needed to be documented for future reference. Only my family and a couple of friends have been told a few things about me, but not a lot. Some things would be hard to believe unless it happens to you. As I am writing this book, there are spirits all around me. They do not talk, just move around me. Last night was the first time I talked to my spirit that was a young girl. I asked her, "Are you okay?" But she did not respond. Although she woke me up like putting something in my mouth. There also was a man in my room and when I looked at him, he backed into my closet, saying not a word. It has taken years to get to this frequency level and a slow journey. From the lady who stood at the foot of my bed at night to the lady touching me. I do not know what's next, only God knows.

I would talk in my sleep to someone every night and wake up screaming and scared. It took me years to recognize that my voice was waking me up and the sound of my voice would frighten me. Through my young years in high school, I would fly in the air. Maybe flying will be my next realization. If I hear a noise that wakes me up and I see them, I just turn over and go back to sleep because they are here to help me, not harm me.

My first notation in my book was that I had just received a call from my new friend Jeff who is such a nice guy. He was conscious of his diet and didn't eat meat and we were also conscious of the wrong that embarked on the Black community. I consider him a good friend of twenty-three years. Jeff wanted me to take some herbs like Alfalfa. I replied by noting in my journal that I wouldn't want to take any. My rule of thumb is to not take any medicine and little herbs. At this point in my life, I needed to generate more male friends and decided Jeff and I could become friends. We celebrated his birthday at the Post, danced a little and talked a lot. For his birthday, I bought him a book to read. After his birthday, I informed Jeff that we should not be friends anymore and that he shouldn't call anymore, and that I wouldn't call him anymore. On November 08, 2000, I am questioning ending our relationship I thought to be very special. Saturday November 11, 2000, I broke down and called Jeff, hoping that after the shady way I treated him he would call me back. Jeff returned my call twice. Once, he left a message and the second time he spoke to my daughter. We finally talked. He said that he wanted to give me some space. As usual he was cordial and respectful, so we tried to continue our relationship.

After I retired, the thing I wanted to do was to have a party to include my family, friends, hometown people and co-workers. This was a special night for me, with lots of food, music, laughter and my newfound friend.

On December 17, 2000, I was awakened by the voice of my mother calling my name. I did not write anything else in my diary until August 13, 2001. I wrote that my stress level was up more than last summer because I had spent the summer keeping my grandsons, Isiah, and Cristian. After retiring to bed early this morning, I heard someone hiccup and I had a feeling that my ancestors would be visiting me. They visited me more often and frightened me so badly I would be scared to go to bed. Tonight, I have communicated with Bobby who had transitioned, but I can't remember the conversation. For the most part if I didn't write it down it would be lost to me. My mind wasn't ready for what was going on with me. On this night, I heard a car drive up in the parking space. Shortly after that, I heard Bobby come in the front door with a woman, talking and playing music, I don't recall the song. I was not asleep and was aware that Bobby was dead. When the music ended, they got quiet. I could still see the shadows on the door. I was thinking I should see what was happening in the front room, but I also was thinking that if he was dead how was he be in the front room? I was semi asleep and completely aware of everything around me. I could view the entire room, the hall to the bathroom and chairs in the rooms, the exit and entrance into the room.

Shortly after I felt a cold chill in my body, although I couldn't see anyone. I heard someone close to me, sniffling as though crying. For some reason I thought it was my mother. I immediately woke up from this semi trance. I had to fight hard to stay out of the trance. I am calling it a trance because I was aware of everything.

One October 14, 2001, I dreamed that I saw James in the tree as I was leaving my house. He had not gone home and was hiding out. I looked back at him, and he disappeared into one of the units. The following day, I told my daughter. On October 16, 2001, my brother called me and told me that James had been taken out of the house where he had lived. My dream showed me that he had been evicted

Monday night, October 15, 2001, I dreamed that I was at work the last day before retirement on the Data site to sign EAR reports. I looked at the calendar and it had 10/15/2000, the EAR reports it had DPP 10. That was the actual data because it was 10/15/2001 and it was DPP 10.

On February 03. 2003, It had been a long time since I wrote in my diary, but my dreams had been so bizarre that I needed to start tracking them. The people in this dream were new to me and began with me looking for a place to buy. In this dream the house was located at Florence and Regent Street. I went across the street to the apartment to get the manager to let me in to see the house. The house was full of people of all ages. The house was nice with a beautiful landscape. I stood and watched them. They appeared to be relatives and came from some town in Mississippi. One lady walked by me and said, "Did she tell you about the train that jumped the track and has hit the house nine times?" This dream was so vivid and as though I was in another time and space. I left the house.

On February 05, 2003, I dreamed I had gone to Washington, DC, for some type of gatherings, can't recall what type of meeting. I was in some theater type of setting, but only can remember bits and pieces of the dream. An unknown white lady was walking with me, but we parted at some point. I continued to walk alone and ended up in a building. Then I would have to exit to continue to the bus station. Outside the door were cops and gangsters. At one point there was a large body of water and a sharp hill too steep to walk down. I had to go down the back way to the bus station.

In a semi dream state on June 27, 2003, fully aware of what was going on, I was hit on top of the head. I saw things and heard noises all around me. On the bed next to my bed was another bed and the shape of the body was like my grandson, Cristian, and I could hear him talking but don't remember what he said. Later in the morning, my daughter told me that Christian had called me for some information regarding our road trip to the Chancellor's family in Montgomery, Alabama.

In my dream today, June 28, 2003, I saw two ladies walk by my bed. They both worked at the post office. One lady worked in human resources that used to appear on the talking drum and the other, I can't remember. The bed I was in was in strange surroundings. It was as if I had been sick and had been on light duty. I also saw Mary walk to my bed, but she didn't speak. My feelings were that they were upset with me and felt like I should be up out of bed and downstairs. I tried to get away from what was happening in the room. Noises were all around my bed from someone sitting on the edge of the bed to something flying. I woke up singing Glory hallelujah since I laid my burden down.

On June 29, 2003, I dreamed of Jack and in the dream, we found out that he liked me and that I didn't like him. I had gone into what looked like a pharmacist to get something for my eyes. The lady put the solution into a container that looked like a scale. At some point, jack came into the room, and we were so glad to see each other. In my dream, he had moved to Los Angeles. It appeared that it was taking a long time to get my eye solution, and I mentioned it to her. Another lady came out to help her, and she poured the solution into a cup and gave it to me to drink whenever I needed it for my eyes. It appeared to me in my dreams that I had used it before in a container used to clear up my eyes. Somehow, he was beside me in bed, and I was talking to him. When I woke up, I was asking him how his family was. This is the first time I can remember the face and the person I was talking to.

On November 20, 2005, I had not written this book since June 29, 2003. My dreams had gotten real. I am talking more and more in my sleep. My dreams have become so real. I see people that I can't recognize in my daily life. I can see these people as I am going to sleep. They are all around as though I am leaving to sleep somewhere else. I wake up a lot of times when I am talking to some, and my own voice wakes me up. It is so frightening to wake me up like this. Sometimes I am angry and shout at the person I am talking to. On November 19, 2005, early Saturday morning I had a strange dream. I had gone into the bedroom where Tam and Isiah sleep, and I saw a shadow at the window as I got closer to the window,

I saw two hands hanging down as if getting ready to come through the top part of the window. Cristian, who was behind me, said I saw some hands. As I got closer, I saw the face of the man. I am not sure what I said to the man, but I think I told the man to come down. I told Chris to get my gun, the man came down from the window and stood to the right of the window. I don't remember him saying anything, but he did have a smile on his face. Today I can still remember what he looked like. This was the first time that I could remember the face of someone that I had talked to that I didn't know.

Today November 20, 05 I had a nice sleep when I woke up, I didn't remember talking in my sleep as I usually do when I woke up my daughter told me that I had talked in my sleep. I told her I didn't remember talking in my sleep, she said she heard me talking to someone and told them that I worked for the post office as a supervisor I was shocked because I remembered that I had talked to a man and that was in my conversation. She said the first part of my conversation was like mumbo jumbo and that she couldn't understand what I was saying. She said the part about me being a supervisor was clear. I don't remember much, but I do remember him coming into my room with a silver spoon in his hand. I was alone feeling uncomfortable and threatened. I explained to him that what I had done was not personal but was for security and that I was a supervisor and that it was my job to provide security although I could not remember what the security was for. Later, other people came into my room, and it was apparent that we had engaged in a prior discussion about him and what he may have done, the man appeared to become more relaxed. I don't remember anything beyond that conversation. Another part of my dream came when I was in the school-type of environment. A woman came in and told me that someone was going to Hawaii as I said, I hope it's not the same people all the time. I am not sure if I wanted to go or not. Later I heard the man tell the teacher we sent her out first they were talking about me. I called them to me, and as they approached me it seemed that I was laying down. The man had on a blue royal suit. I told them that I had heard what they had said about me, also the teacher had graded the tests, but I had not received my grade,

On July 27,2706 in the morning, I felt the presence of someone to the right side of my face and then I saw a man on the left side of my body looking at me, He had a big white shirt on. My feelings were that he was in good spirits therefore I was not afraid. This man reminded me of the young man who worked at Simply Wholesome. Later that day when I was coming out of Walmart's I saw a young man with baggy pants on and a large white shirt. Seeing this man triggered my dream this morning.

July 24,2006 Monday evening around 4:30 p.m. or 5:00 p.m. I was reading a letter that had been sent to me. I started to feel ill all over and as I was reading the letter and watching the TV at the same time my vision became jumbled up. I turn the TV off and laid down, but it got worst. I prayed for healing and thought I was going blind. I wanted to call one of my children, I was so frightened. I decided to go to the emergency room and have my eyes checked and I started to call 911. As I was walking out the door to go to the emergency room, my vision started to clear up. My prayers were answered.

Monday Morning approx. 3:45 am I woke up with pain in my lower abdomen and my legs were up. I went to the bathroom and my vision started to show double again. I felt like something was in my left eye. I laid down but was too dizzy, so I sat up until the dizziness went away. This whole thing lasted about 20 minutes. It was so frightening, and I prayed to God to help me.

August 02, 2006, Wednesday morning I did a lot of talking to someone and at the time I knew who I was talking to. I woke up on my right, talking with my hands in motion. It could have been Bobby, I can't remember. At another point I was on my back, and I believe I was talking to a man who walked in the back of the bed and pushed it down I can't remember now but at that time I knew who it was. When I woke up, I saw a spider crawling beside me on the wall.

Last week—I don't know the date—I was sleeping in the bed, and I saw something that scared me so bad I remember sitting straight up in the bed. Later that morning I was washing dishes as I turned around and saw a big bug coming through the door at the top. I ran to the door and put the mop on it and closed the door to keep it from coming into the house. It was at the top of the door crawling in when I took the mop down it fell and I pushed it out of the porch, I saw the correlation between the incident and the one with the spider.

August 09, 2006, woke up and sat straight up in the bed. I had screamed; I remember talking to someone before I heard myself scream. I remember hoping no one had heard me screaming. Before this, when I woke up screaming, I would have seen something that was so frightening. Monday morning, I saw a big black bug crawling on the floor it looked like a cricket when I hit it flew up in the air and disappeared it shortly appeared again, I killed it.

August 16, 2006, found some notes that I had written in another book dated April 29, 30, 2006. Someone woke me up by touching my left hand. On May 1, 2006, I felt the pressure of something or someone in my presence. I was fighting not to go to sleep.

September 19, 2006, one of my daughters called out to mama, and I woke up. It was about (5:35 am).

September 30, 2006, on a Friday morning my mid-morning dream was so vivid. When I woke up it was about 2:45 a.m. I was in bed and aware that I was lying down it also appeared as though I was pretending that I was asleep or maybe I was sick. People were coming back to check on me I remember Jack's voice but can't remember what he said. I looked from the bed and saw people lined up in the room. I saw someone talking to someone who looked like Betty, my co-worker, and then some woman looked at me and said she is awake or something I can't remember. I started moving my body and making signs to let them know I was okay. I started to sing this song and when I woke up crying and singing this song. My Lord, He calls me. I don't have long to stay here. He calls me like thunder, the trumpet sounds within my soul I don't have time to stay here I don't have long to stay here.

11/16/2006 I just recently started to sleep better and during the night My dreams are vivid are coming back and I am talking, and they are talking to me. I woke up this morning with Kaia in my mind. I was thinking that I would take her shopping when I got there as opposed to taking her a box of things. Bobby called me this morning to tell me that Kaia had dreamed about me this morning around 1:00 a.m. And she sat straight up in bed.

Saturday 01/20 2007 between the hours of 9:30 a.m. and 10:00 a.m. I was in the first bedroom at the top of the stairs because I wanted to get some sunshine. The sun was bright and shining directly into the room. I wanted to look directly into the sun so that my eyesight would improve. As I looked directly into the sunlight. I began to blink, seeing vibrant orange colors. There were two round objects on each side of the sun.

As I continued to look at the sun, it continued to vibrate, and little orange sun rays were approaching me coming right behind each other into the windows onto the bed. I would give a count of five or six and they were about one-half feet apart. At this point, I was truly afraid. To get away I headed downstairs but saw one on the patio door. As I settled down, I went back upstairs and attempted to look at the sun again, but it was too bright a star-like color. Later that night I went on the Internet to look up planets and to see which planet could be seen with the naked I the sun picture was on the Internet and the same color that I had seen by the objects/sunrays that I had seen the objects/sunrays that had entered and was on my bed.

Prior to seeing the sun vibrate that morning, I had closed my eyes and looked at the sun. I could see two black dots as they became clearer; I believe they reflected me. I also had seen the eyes on Friday while looking at the sun with my eyes closed. My dream state that night was somewhat blurry. I woke up during the night trying to get out of bed. I thought about where I was going and hoped that I hadn't walked in my sleep. It dawned on me that I was either getting into or out of bed. I forgot the whole thing, but for sure, I was in my dream.

January 28, 2007. In looking at the sun today, I see the sun and three planets to the left of the sun and two planets to the right of the sun. The sun has now moved to the east. I also see dark yellow orange images in the windows, on the blinds, in my book where I was writing on my hands and my body. To make sure that I wasn't getting a reflection, I raised the blinds so that only the window was visible.

June 8, 2008, as I was driving in the afternoon, my left eye started to lose vision, something seems to first the corner of my eye and then move to the middle of both eyes. Both eyes were dimmed and so I pulled off the road for a minute but started up again because I needed to get home. It lasted for about fifteen to twenty minutes, and I was okay.

September 27, 2011, into Tuesday morning I, woke up singing red, white and Blue from Louie Armstrong song It's a wonderful world. Later that morning I, saw two rainbows on the wall and ceiling. One was over by my bed. I tried to think of what exactly I was seeing until yesterday (September 28, 2011) that I had been listening to "Over the Rainbow." Confirmation of the power of the mind.

December 6, 2011. Early morning, I dreamed I was an Egyptian Queen. I was dead and had come alive. Strange dream. I looked up information and saw that we had a lot in common.

10/17/2012 I experienced eye problems again for about 30 minutes in both eyes. It was like I, was going blind. I was washing dishes and started to see multiple colors that resemble when my TV started to act up. I had to lay down at least two times. I closed my eyes and prayed for healing, and I could feel my eyes returning to normal.

10/19/2012 4:30 p.m. I am having this eye experience again. It is worse than before. All these mixed colors looked like a puzzle with very fast movements. I lay down until around 4:50 p.m. and my eyes were better, but I had a headache.

Tuesday June 28, 2014, I believe I traveled to South Africa. In my dream, I was highly concerned that I was there. Two of my daughters were there also. My daughter was getting sick because she had not drunk any water prior to our traveling. I remember asking an African lady for water, and it was priced at $200.00 a bottle. I also remember looking at the sky and seeing something moving very fast don't know if it was an airplane. I also saw a Chevron gas station and we walked there because the gas was cheaper.

03/22/19 I Dreamed that a big bear was running to me and playing with my left hand for some reason I wasn't afraid of the bear.

Since I was a child with the Pretty lady that stood at the foot of my bed, I have come through several frequencies. I called them awareness You may call your changes another name. My experiences, I believe, are not unique. People just don't talk about them. There are still things I don't discuss with my children. Since I initiated this book, I felt it was time to tell my story, regardless of who believed me or not. I refused to allow anyone to insert or change anything I had written. My diary is directly connected to my dreams and actual events. As of now, I have not been given permission to share the information or events that are currently Hopefully, by the time this book is published I will have an answer.

Pictorial

United States Postal Service

is conferred upon

Viola Chancellor

in recognition of notable performance

LOS ANGELES
dated at

OCTOBER 15, 1992
on

C. W. KING
GENERAL MANAGER/POSTM

CARVER HIGH SCHOOL
CLASS OF 1960